PRIVATE SYDNEY

First Published by Scriptum Editions

565 Fulham Road, London, SW6 1ES

Created by Co & Bear Productions (UK) Ltd

Copyright © 2000 Co & Bear Productions (UK) Ltd

Photographs copyright © 2000 Willem Rethmeier

Publisher Beatrice Vincenzini

Executive Director David Shannon

Editorial Director Alexandra Black

Art Director David Mackintosh

Printed and bound in Italy
at Officine Grafiche De Agostini

First edition
10 9 8 7 6 5 4 3 2 1

ISBN 1-902686-11- x

PRIVATE
SYDNEY

PHOTOGRAPHED BY WILLEM RETHMEIER

WRITTEN BY JENNA REED BURNS

SCRIPTUM EDITIONS
LONDON · HONG KONG

CONTENTS

INTRODUCTION

Although it's Australia's oldest and largest city, Sydney is one of the world's youngest metropolises. It is also one of the most naturally beautiful. Situated on the eastern coast of the continent, it is bound to the east by the blue waters of the Tasman Sea, to the north by the sandstone escarpments of the Hawkesbury River, to the south by the Royal National Park (the world's second oldest national park), and to the west by the aptly named Blue Mountains, part of the Great Dividing Range. But what gives the city its energetic, exuberant and extroverted character is the water — a spectacular working harbour, and an almost unbroken line of exquisite ocean beaches that fringe the coast.

Water is also the subject matter for an all-important element of Sydney life: views. Sydney is a city that runs on the hot topic of real estate. Who has bought, who has sold and the seemingly ever-upward spiral of real-estate prices are recurring topics at dinner parties around town. Although the population centre is now situated somewhere west of Parramatta (originally an inland settlement), the most affluent suburbs are those that overlook the harbour.

The harbour and the oldest bridge which crosses it (the Sydney Harbour Bridge, known affectionately as 'The Coathanger') effectively divide the city into many smaller communities. To the north, the eastern shore is split into the salubrious suburbs of the lower north shore (Neutral Bay, Cremorne and Mosman) and the leafy upper north shore. In the former you'll find wide, tree-lined streets with grand, old, brick houses, many of them built around the time of Federation (1900), which has lent its name to their architectural style. It's the domain of established families.

Its streets are full of expensive shops and the area is dotted with exclusive private schools.

Further north, the houses are generally of a younger vintage, though built on larger blocks

land full of mature exotic and native trees which attract abundant birdlife. Bordering the

ihern surf beaches are middle-class suburbs of unassuming bungalows; however, the bushy tip

of the peninsula which juts into Pittwater and Broken Bay is generally considered to be holiday territory. Palm Beach is where wealthy Sydneysiders have whiled away their weekends since the 1920s.

Returning to the harbour, the central business district immediately south of the bridge marks the distinction between the classy eastern suburbs of Darling Point, Bellevue Hill, Woollahra and Paddington, and the trendy inner-west (Balmain, Glebe, Newtown and Leichhardt).

The eastern suburbs are a mix of grand old houses and ostentatious new houses (built as older ones are demolished); however, Paddington is renowned for its

BELOW

The view from Lavender Bay, with the white sails of the Sydney Opera House framed by the Sydney Harbour Bridge.

serried rows of lacy Victorian terrace houses and village-like atmosphere. It attracts young professional couples, who enjoy the area's café society and spend their weekends shopping in the fashionable boutiques that line one side of Oxford Street. Further east is Bondi, replete with squat 1940s blocks of flats and semi-detached houses with tiled red roofs. Its famous beach has

attracted a casual beachside culture, which has spread down the coast into the neighbouring sub-

urbs of Bronte, Coogee and Clovelly.

On the other side of the city, the once-gritty inner-west is slowly being gentrified. The original

old houses (a mix of Victorian terraces, freestanding Federation houses, post war bungalows and

weatherboard workers' cottages) are being restored and

renovated. Locals claim it's a more interesting part

of town because of the lively socio-economic mix —

generations of migrants rub shoulders with older working-

class residents, students, academics, young professionals

and ordinary families.

The city sprawls west all the way to the Blue Mountains,

where national parks of rugged and spectacular beauty are

bisected by settled areas — a century ago, the destination

for holidaying city folk, but now outer suburbs of Sydney

itself. South of the city there are more beachside suburbs,

while the waterways of Georges River and Port Hacking have created areas of new affluence.

As for styles of architecture and interior design found both near the harbour and further

afield, they are many and varied, as is testified by the selection of houses within this book.

For decades, Australian architects, builders and developers followed the styles set by Europe and, in particular, England. Houses faced the street as social convention dictated, and many were dark inside, with small poky rooms. Few were suited to Sydney's climate: they were stuffy, hot boxes in summer and cold, dreary places in winter.

Gradually, however, as the country begins to forge its own identity, a unique Australian style of architecture is taking shape — one that better responds to the landscape and the climate, and utilises in new and interesting ways what are often thought to be local building materials, such as corrugated iron and fibro cement board, as well as native hardwood timbers and glass.

At the same time, older-style houses have regained an appreciative younger audience because of their decorative architectural features (and usually their close proximity to the city). They are being renovated to suit the climate and today's lifestyles better, with open-plan living areas added to the rear and a reorientation towards the light and, of course, views if they exist.

Most first-time visitors to Australia comment on the strength of the light, and it is one of the greatest influences on Australian architecture and design. The brightness of the strong southern-hemisphere sunlight also allows for a much stronger palette than is used in northern Europe. Here the pretty pastels of England can appear washed out and sickly.

Sydney's temperate weather means that natural cross-ventilation and an easy flow from indoors to outdoors are additional sought-after features. Gardens are no longer just green places to potter about in, but must contain areas for outdoor entertaining, as well as rest and relaxation.

OPPOSITE

One of Sydney's many ferries chugs across the harbour on its way from Neutral Bay, on the lower north shore, to Circular Quay. Rising up behind the Royal Botanical Gardens and the Sydney Opera House are the tall skyscrapers of the city's central business district.

OPPOSITE & BELOW

The Sydney Opera House was designed by the Danish architect, Jørn Utzon. The sails of gleaming-white ceramic tiles were inspired by the segments of an orange. Its position on the eastern coast of the continent means that Sydney is edged with numerous sandy surf beaches.

With the increasing pressures of modern urban life, houses and their gardens must function as private sanctuaries at the day's end. Decorating styles vary, reflecting the personalities of different owners — from starkly minimal, to quirky and eclectic or grand and opulent. As one of the most multicultural cities in the world, all aspects of Sydney life reflect the ethnic diversity of the population. Just as the cuisine fuses Asian, Mediterranean and other ethnic influences to create an individual style, the common feature of Sydney interiors is their hybrid nature. People mix and match styles with ease, creating generally relaxed, informal interiors that suit their way of life. Tribal art sits beside fine porcelain; gilded antiques add depth and patina to contemporary surrounds. Because of the manner in which the country was settled and the nature of the people who settled there, it has probably always been thus, and it is this heterogeneous approach which creates a style that is distinctly Sydney.

Living

1

by the Water

SUMMER BREEZE

· [EASTERN SUBURBS]

ABOVE

During the day, light filters down through the void from a skylight in the roof above the entrance foyer.

OPPOSITE

A deep, colonnaded verandah wraps around the front and side of the house, providing a sheltered vantage point from where to admire the view.

S ydney is a city that runs on the hot topic of real estate, and this house (in an exclusive harbourside suburb) has long been one of the stars. A particularly colourful period of its history occurred in the 1970s when, as a private hotel, it became the haunt of visiting rock stars.

From the street the house resembles an Italian villa, but hidden behind the classical façade are the bones of a smaller Victorian Italianate house. The original turret and parapet work are the only obvious remnants. The rest of the house has been altered many times during its life — most recently by architects William Zuccon and Espie Dods, with interiors designed by Thomas Hamel, who collaborated with Janie Marshall to realise the owners' vision.

The exterior colour (seashell pink, with green louvred shutters) gives some indication of the departure from decorative convention that lies inside. It's not that the interior is unconventional — rather that it's a fresh, youthful take on opulent style. The owners, originally from Melbourne, favour pure, clear colours. In Hamel's opinion, they also understand old houses and know how to adapt them to suit today's lifestyles and the needs of a family.

Once inside the elaborate cast-iron gates and through the front door, it's obvious that the limestone-paved, oval entrance foyer has a Georgian sensibility. A sweeping cantilevered staircase leading up to the first floor is off to one side, edged with the same elegant black-iron balustrade that encircles the gallery directly overhead. The architecture is decidedly gracious, but the pink walls add a touch of playfulness, therefore diffusing the formality.

Ahead is a glimpse of the view through the family room, and off to the left is a double

dining and sitting room. The two formal rooms complement each other faultlessly. The red walls of the dining room are a rich foil for a collection of silver and glass, while the apple green of the living room is the ideal backdrop for yellow-upholstered furniture and cushions in mixed prints.

The vivacious interior almost vies with the view for attention. Through the windows the land falls away in a series of terraces down to the harbour's edge. Limestone stairs lead from the lawn to a timber deck surrounding the pool. Along one side is a quaint timber boathouse. With French doors opening onto the deck on two sides, it's the perfect place to sit and watch the sunset.

The close proximity to the water, accompanied by the briny smell of the sea and the sound of rigging jangling against the masts of the yachts moored nearby, gives visitors the sense that they, too, are floating on the harbour. Complete with bedroom, bathroom, kitchenette and a sitting room, the boathouse is the ideal guest accommodation. Being adjacent to the swimming pool also means that the owners' three children use it when entertaining their friends.

The owners themselves entertain regularly, hosting a range of functions at the house. It's therefore not surprising to find a slickly organised, commercial-grade kitchen inside. Beside it is a casual dining area overlooking a courtyard garden and terrace sheltered by a wisteria-covered pergola. Although ostensibly for family meals, this pretty lemon-coloured room, with its French oak parquetry floor, is the chosen venue for small, informal lunches. Like the rest of the interior, the feeling is fresh and lively, and in summer the heady citrus scent of two *magnolia grandifloras* in bloom across the courtyard strikes exactly the right accompanying note.

OPPOSITE

The gallery above the entrance foyer and the stair leading up to it are edged with a voluptuously curved, cast-iron balustrade, designed by architect William Zuccon and forged by Hans Schappi.

ABOVE

An antique runner adds warmth to the limestone floor of the hallway, while a Houndi lamp casts a warm glow over a collection of oil paintings, reflected in the mirror on the opposite wall.

LEFT & ABOVE

The boathouse was reroofed with copper and painted a soft pink to match the house. The interior is lined with limed timber boards, with transparent lace curtains at the windows to soften the edges. The indoor–outdoor Brown Jordan and antique Lloyd Loom furniture can be pulled out onto the pool deck if required. The glass-and-metal star lantern comes from England.

ABOVE LEFT

The walls of the dining room are papered in vibrant red wallpaper, which provides
the perfect foil for the clients' collection of antique nautical paintings. The large
extendable dining table can seat up to twenty people for a formal dinner party.

ABOVE RIGHT & OPPOSITE

A collection of porcelain birds by Anne Gordon, a UK ceramicist, sits beside an
antique French clock on the marble sitting-room mantelpiece. A Hepplewhite
sofa sits at one end of the room, with its back to the balcony. Behind is a
Georgian grandfather clock flanked by draped French doors.

OPPOSITE

The long island bench in the kitchen is lit by an overhanging light fitting, designed by Thomas Hamel. A custom-designed plate rack is mounted on the wall above the sink, and a collection of antique porcelain plates decorates the wall above the adjacent cooking areas.

LEFT

A casual dining room runs off the slickly organised kitchen where Sofie, the springer spaniel, lies waiting for dinner. A French Provincial table is surrounded by chairs with apple-green legs and checked slipcovers for easy laundering. Above the table hangs a nickel-plated, Dutch-style chandelier.

RIGHT

The walls of the downstairs guest
bedroom are upholstered in a Colefax
& Fowler fabric, as a homage to New
York decorator Mark Hampton, who
used the same fabric in his own sitting
room. In the hallway outside a low
chest on a stand bears a collection
of Staffordshire porcelain.

OPPOSITE

The view from the window across
the harbour takes in one of the city's
iconic structures – Sydney Harbour
Bridge. The walls of the upstairs guest
bedroom are upholstered in the same
toile fabric used for the curtains.
An antique, French barometer hangs
on the wall above the desk.

ARTISTIC CONVERSION

· [LOWER NORTH SHORE]

ABOVE & OPPOSITE

The attic bedroom, reached by a spiral staircase in the tower, is a wonderful study in white on white, creating a soothing ethereal space high above the tree tops. Joel Ellenberg's unfinished marble sculpture of Wendy rests on the floor of the bedroom.

As one of the curators at the Art Gallery of New South Wales puts it, walking into the Lavender Bay house where artist Brett Whiteley lived and worked for fifteen years feels like walking into one of his paintings. Since the artist's untimely death of a drug overdose some eight years ago, his stature and importance in both the local and international art world has continued to grow. A legendary dimension has been added to his memory, and in this house his presence feels almost tangible because of the number of original paintings and drawings hanging in the very rooms that are featured in so many of them.

The airy downstairs room that was for a long time his second studio retains the sense of an artist's workroom. (Brett Whiteley's main studio in Surry Hills, where he moved to full time in 1988, is now open to the public, and features constantly changing exhibitions.) However, the house has also always been very much his wife Wendy's personal domain. A constant work-in-progress, the interior elements are now regularly rearranged according to which works are being lent to the studio or various travelling exhibitions.

When Brett and Wendy Whiteley returned to Sydney with their daughter Arkie after ten years overseas, they moved into a vacant flat on the first floor of the house. A few years later, the owner decided to sell and he offered them first option.

The house — the end terrace of a row of five two-storey Federation terraces built in a harbourside park — was typical of its style, with lots of small dark rooms and lead-light windows. Like many older houses, it didn't make the most of its greatest asset — a view across Lavender Bay

and the harbour, framed by the Harbour Bridge and Luna Park on one side and Blues Point promontory on the other. The Whiteleys opened up the house by removing doors and knocking out walls, replacing them with arches, which they rendered roughly and then painted white. A master bedroom was created in the attic and for a long time was accessible only by ladder until a tower, enclosing a spiral staircase, was added to one side of the house to link all three levels.

With the purchase of their first house after years of a nomadic existence came the security of ownership and a sense of coming home. This infused Brett Whiteley's work, and the following years are credited with being among his finest. Lavender Bay and Sydney Harbour became the subjects of many of his paintings from this time, most of which emanate a feeling of joy and peace.

Lately Wendy Whiteley has been renovating. Cracks in the living-room walls have been filled and the kauri floorboards have received another coat of white paint. Structural work required to shore up the foundations exposed enough room under the house for a cellar-like guest bedroom, with exposed sandstone walls and French doors that lead directly out to the park through cast-iron gates bearing her initials. There are plans to extend the kitchen and create a dining area, as well as to add an en-suite bathroom to the upstairs bedroom.

Even with these changes, the house will remain a curious pastiche of styles: old and new, Mediterranean and tribal, with a dash of Asia thrown in for good measure. But the overriding impression is one of light and space, a serene world floating up amongst the tree tops, allowing Wendy Whiteley to maintain an enviable level of peace.

OPPOSITE & ABOVE
French doors from the newly excavated guest room under the house open onto a small paved forecourt. A pair of cast-iron gates bearing Wendy Whiteley's initials lead directly out to the adjacent harbourside park.

OPPOSITE & ABOVE

One of Brett Whiteley's **Giraffe** *sculptures (***Giraffe 1***) stands on a plinth in the corner of the garden. Its elongated shape is echoed by that of the tower containing the spiral staircase behind. The top of the tower affords a spectacular view across the harbour to the Bridge and Luna Park, situated on Milsons Point. An even better view of the park can be seen from a window in the front gable of the attic bedroom and enjoyed from the window seat covered in crisp white linen cushions.*

LEFT & ABOVE

On the first floor, a large open-plan living space opens directly onto a balcony.
Wendy Whiteley pulled the large carved lion out of a ditch in Bali many years ago
and freighted it home. Above it hangs Brett Whiteley's Blue River with Egg, while
over the seventeenth-century chest on the left hangs his Lavender Bay at Night,
which features one of the large date palms that fringe the path through the park
outside. When the cracks in the living-room walls were repaired recently, Wendy
liked the glimpses of original paint and decided to leave them exposed for a while.

ABOVE

Whiteley's **Dead Dingo** features a mummified dingo encased in a Perspex box
hanging on the studio wall. Three small New Guinea sculptures and an African
monkey sculpture on an organ stand keep it company on the mantelpiece.

RIGHT

Brett Whiteley created a second studio in what originally would have been the
main living room of the house. His large canvas, **Two Giraffes**, which was painted
for an exhibition in London, in 1962, dominates the space that is now used as a
guest room. Next to it is his **Giraffe 2** sculpture, with a New Guinea spear and
two New Guinea carvings alongside.

ABOVE

Brett Whiteley's charcoal drawing, The Willow Tree, catches the light streaming
through a front door in the open-plan living area. The spiral staircase in the tower
can be glimpsed through the doorway. The long oak refectory table in the
foreground is eighteenth-century English – propped at one end is part of a marble
sculpture by Joel Ellenberg, who was a close friend of the Whiteleys.

OPPOSITE

A new guest bedroom, with exposed sandstone walls, has been created in the space
under the house. Its effect has been to ground the house, providing direct access
through French doors on one side to the harbourside park beyond the gates. The
exposed aggregate concrete floor is heated by electric underfloor cables, and an
industrial, stainless-steel locker provides wardrobe space.

OPPOSITE & ABOVE

Wendy Whiteley's dressing room is filled with her wonderful array of scarfs and
wraps, hatboxes and jewellery, all laid out on the bench as if for an exhibition.
Two old wooden shoe lasts sit beside some Japanese lacquerware, silver jewellery,
and a collection of blue and white ceramics which were all hand-painted by Brett
Whiteley. On top of the chest of drawers various other pieces of china from Wendy
Whiteley's collection sit in front of two Rajasthani wood carvings .

HARBOURSIDE HACIENDA

· [ELIZABETH BAY]

ABOVE

Beneath the colourful Cordova-tile roof, the eaves are supported by navy-blue, shaped eave brackets.

OPPOSITE

Two wall candle sconces in the form of swords by Mark Brazier-Jones hang in the guest-house dining room. They were so admired by Janet Jackson when filming a commercial at the house that she implored the owners to sell them to her. They had to recommission another pair from the artist.

S ince it was built in the late 1920s for the (then) phenomenal sum of £60,000, Elizabeth Bay's Boomerang has remained the most expensive Sydney residence. Built for the music publisher and harmonica manufacturer Frank Albert, the house was named after his popular songbooks and range of mouth organs. The Aboriginal motif appears throughout the house: over the entry gate, in the twin wall fountains of the porte-cochère, on two sundials in the garden, in a bas-relief carving on the fireplace in the entrance foyer, and on the chimney breast of the library fireplace. When the swimming pool was built in 1984, the motif was incorporated into the tiling.

The current owners, Sally and Duncan Mount, are the sixth since the property was first sold. The fact that Albert lived in the house until his death in 1962 (when a caretaker looked after the property for a further sixteen years before it was sold), as well as a recently applied heritage order, has helped to preserve the building and its extensive grounds. And Sydney is all the richer for it.

The house, with its opulent finishes and fine craftsmanship, is of inestimable value. Variously described as Spanish Mission, Spanish Hacienda style, Hollywood Spanish Revival, and Spanish American style, it brought the Hispanic style of architecture that is so favoured by Hollywood to Australia and gave it immediate cachet.

Designed by little-known English-born architect Neville Hampson, the house created a sensation when it was built. It is lavishly detailed, both inside and out. Arrival is through cast-iron gates, which open onto a brick-paved carriage-loop that passes through an elegant porte-cochère. The front garden is divided into two distinct areas: directly in front of the house is a large

rectangular tiled pool with a fountain; and to the east is a shady courtyard, a neat grid of paving stones and mondo grass. Along one edge, a wisteria-covered pergola leads to a smaller two-storey building, once a garage with accommodation for the chauffeur, but now used as an office and garage, with sumptuous guest quarters above.

Returning to the house, the arched front door is fitted with cast-iron gates. A pair of bevelled glass doors lead into a small vestibule that acts as an airlock, with another pair of matching doors opening into a grand entrance foyer. An elliptical void allows a glimpse of the first-floor gallery above. The wide staircase leading up to the bedrooms is washed in red and blue light as sun filters through lead-light windows on the landing. A narrower stair descends to a cinema, playroom, laundry and various storage areas, located in the basement.

On the other side of the entrance foyer is the drawing room. To its left is the oak-panelled library with a Tudor-style feature fireplace, while to the right is the most exquisite room in terms of finishes. Every surface of the dining room, apart from the floor, is completely hand-carved in mahogany, including the coffered ceiling, the elaborate wall panelling and fluted columns.

The property extends to the harbour's edge. In front of the house is a wide brick-paved terrace and a flight of stairs leading to the lawn and pool. To the west, tucked beside the house, is a sheltered Moroccan-style courtyard with a loggia defining its edge.

The Hollywood Spanish Revival style was associated with fun, sun and leisure. Boomerang epitomises all of that, but includes a hefty dose of fantasy as well.

OPPOSITE

The pool is aligned with the main axis of the house. Two urns on pedestals and a pair of striped German timber canvas chairs flank the stairs leading from the terrace to the lawn.

BELOW

'Boomerang' appears in the tiling of the base of the pool. The 'M' and 'R' of the word are highlighted as they were (conveniently) the initials of the owner, who installed the pool in 1984.

LEFT & ABOVE

Unlike many waterfront properties in Sydney, the sea wall marks the front

boundary of Boomerang. The front, north-facing garden is dominated by the pool

set into the lawn. Eight freestanding lamps set into the lawn are original, and mark

the position of the original pathways, which divided the garden into four quarters,

with a sundial at the central intersection. The sundial has been moved into the

palm grove in the far corner of the garden. A launch waits alongside a small jetty

on the other side of the sea wall at the bottom of the garden.

RIGHT

A herringbone-patterned brick-paved terrace provides an extensive outdoor entertaining area in front of the house. A long slab of Swiss marble forms an outdoor table, and is surrounded by unusual Italian wrought-wire chairs.

BELOW

There are many architectural elements of Boomerang that give it a Spanish appearance, such as the brightly glazed Córdoba roof tiles, rendered exterior, arched doorways and elaborate iron grilles over windows and doors.

FAR LEFT

The western courtyard garden has a decidedly Islamic feel. It features an arcaded loggia (with Córdoba roof tiles) around the perimeter and a sunken area in the centre, reached via a set of circular stone steps. In the centre of the courtyard is a tiled octagonal pool, one of several similar pools in different areas of the garden. The courtyard was originally planted with banana palms, but is now home to four Livistonia palms and a quartet of clipped bay trees, which stand around the fountain.

LEFT

A Moroccan wall fountain emphasises the courtyard's Moorish influences.

OPPOSITE

Two wrought-iron gates leading from the drawing room feature a pair of peacocks perched on urns. This has led the owners to refer to it as the Peacock Room – a description further enhanced by the elegant fanlights. Elaborate plaster finishes resembling stone clad the walls to picture-rail height, and the green and cream chequered floor tiles are thought to be made from compressed wood chips.

LEFT

The floor of the porte-cochère is tiled with mosaics, which match those used in the pair of wall fountains that flank the entrance-way. The front doorway consists of three sets of arched doors. Behind the cast-iron grille, a pair of bevelled glass doors open into a small vestibule that serves as an airlock, with another set of doors leading into the entrance foyer. Circular steps in the oak parquet floor of the drawing room are defined with inlaid ebony marquetry.

LEFT

An elliptical void above the circular entrance hall allows a visual link between the ground and first floors. There is some contention over the material used to pave the entrance foyer. Some experts believe it to be travertine (possibly laid with its unpolished side up); others think it is artificial, a pseudo-stucco called 'staff' that was invented in France in the late nineteenth century as a cheaper alternative to marble.

ABOVE

The magnificent main staircase has a wrought-iron balustrade with peacock-tail design. A massive fireplace in the entrance hall, made from artificial stone, features a carved bas-relief detail of Aborigines carrying boomerangs.

ABOVE & OPPOSITE

It is rumoured that the walls of the drawing room were originally upholstered in elephant skin. Now they are clad in a more ecologically friendly, pale-grey, water-marked silk taffeta. An oak-panelled library with a Tudor-style feature fireplace, modelled in artificial stone, leads off the drawing room. A seventeenth-century Flemish tapestry hangs above the stairway leading to the first floor. The afternoon sun filters through the stained-glass window, washing the walls with coloured light.

FAR & NEAR RIGHT

Every surface of the dining room (except the floor) features hand-carved mahogany. On one side of the room is a built-in cabinet, and on the other a built-in sideboard with a revolving servery above, which can be accessed from the butler's pantry next door.

BELOW RIGHT

A bejewelled Daum glass vase by Garouste & Bonnetti from France sits between two antique gilded candelabras on the dining table.

LEFT

The ground floor of the guest house,
adjacent to the garage, is filled with
exotic furniture created by Mark
Brazier-Jones. The illuminated area
in the floor beneath the green chaise
longue, in front of an atmospheric
three-panelled mural, was the original
vehicle-inspection pit in the garage,
which was also fitted out with a
petrol pump, crane and hoist.

LEFT & ABOVE

The opulent bathroom in the guest house was created to replicate the en-suite

bathroom of the master bedroom. The formula to create the crystal glazing on the

lapis lazuli wall tiles was sourced in America, but the tiles were made in Australia.

The process involved growing crystals on the tiles as they were fired in the kilns,

and took many months of trial and error. The creamy-gold wall tiles in the

downstairs cloakroom in the main house feature the same crystal pattern.

FAIRWEATHER FRIEND

· [EASTERN BEACHES]

ABOVE

A Balinese teak bench, which sits permanently out on the rear deck, has been bleached by the sun.

OPPOSITE

The exterior of the house was once quite run-down. The current owners began by restoring the original weatherboards, recladding the roof with clean blue corrugated iron and installing a new picket fence with Western Australian limestone pillars.

When people speak of falling in love with a house, they are often referring to the intangible but overwhelming feeling of goodwill they experienced when first entering it. Occasionally specific features are singled out, but rarely is the kitchen sink identified as the salient feature. Shannon Brookes, however, is not at all embarrassed to admit that the old, pale-blue enamel kitchen sink and draining board were what convinced both her and her husband to buy this charming weatherboard fisherman's cottage in 1995. Along with the sink, she also lists the original kitchen hearth, and a palm that arches over the rear deck, as deciding factors.

Her attitude to the tree, the hearth and the kitchen sink sums up her sensitive approach towards the house. Her respect for its age and the form it has acquired over time, as well as the various qualities that are integral to the spirit of the place, makes a refreshing change in a developer-driven and avaricious city such as Sydney.

Brookes and her husband Michael were drawn to the suburb for similar reasons. Watsons Bay is a small beachside community, a twenty-minute drive from the city proper, and one of the last character-filled pockets in Sydney. Originally settled by fishermen, who moored their boats in the bay, most of the houses are weatherboard cottages built around the turn of the century. Many of today's residents are the children of those original fishermen, and their continued presence has helped preserve the close-knit character of the tiny network of streets that makes up the suburb.

Brookes likens living in her fisherman's cottage to being on holiday seven days a week. With timber lining boards cladding both internal walls and ceilings, the house has an honest,

simple air. No surface is strictly plumb and the house creaks with the wind and changes in

humidity. Its slightly rickety nature appealed to Brookes, who grew up in a high-rise apartment.

She talks about the sense of space and freedom she felt when moving into the house, and one

of the first things she had installed in the garden was a rotating clothes line — only a native-born

flat-dweller could derive so much delight from such a ubiquitous and commonplace invention.

The house has endured several renovations over its 100 years of existence, and Brookes

felt the need to draw together all of the disparate elements to give the house a sense of cohesive-

ness. Her natural stylistic inclination is towards the casual and the eclectic — mixing old with new,

and throwing in ethnic flavours from the Meditteranean region (Portuguese, Moroccan, Greek) —

which, happily, worked well with what the previous owners had done. She deliberately reduced

the palette of materials, using the pigmented polished concrete of the floor downstairs as the

material for the new kitchen and barbecue worktops.

Although a lot of work was done to the outside of the house to improve its appearance

(including stripping away the fibro cladding to reveal the original weatherboards, and replacing

the heavy roof tiles with sky blue corrugated iron), most of the changes Brookes has wrought are

minimal — just some careful tweaking and thoughtful improvements on what was already there.

It's an approach that is perfectly in keeping with her stated objective: never to lose sight of

what appealed to her about the house in the first place. Needless to say, the kitchen hearth,

Canary Island palm tree and pale-blue enamel kitchen sink all remain.

ABOVE

A metal Moroccan-style lamp hangs in
the hallway, which has walls clad with
timber lining boards. The custom made
front door has built-in shutters.

OPPOSITE

A chequered blue and white rug
dresses up a plain blade wall
separating the living area from
the stairwell leading down to the
bedrooms and bathrooms.

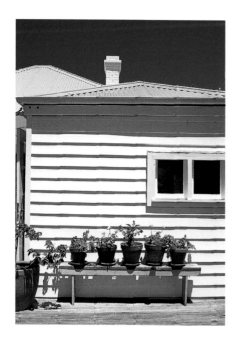

RIGHT

The owner wanted to make a feature of the barbecue because of its iconic status in backyard Australia, but also so it could serve as an extension to the kitchen. Pigmented concrete is used for the worktop outside, and on top of a wooden bench stand terracotta pots filled with scarlet geraniums.

OPPOSITE

The rear, north-facing deck, which leads directly off the living area and the kitchen, is an extension of the living space and is used for meals when the weather is fine. A sail-shaped awning strung above the doors shades the house from the hot summer sun.

OPPOSITE

The old kitchen fireplace was another reason the owner fell in love with the cottage, and she was adamant that it had to stay in any redesign of the room. Fitted with cupboard doors, it now provides extra storage space. The original pale-blue enamel sink was also relocated to a spot beneath the window.

ABOVE

An internal wall has been removed to create one large, open-plan living and dining area that spans the full width of the house. The original wide Oregon floorboards have been treated with an oil-and-woodwash mixture that colours them softly while nourishing the timber.

ABOVE

The blade walls behind the two washbasins conceal a toilet on one side and

a shower on the other. A large, glazed, turquoise pot sits in a niche in the wall,

emphasising the room's Mediterranean ambience. Beside the master suite, the

open risers of the staircase leading up to the main floor are reflected in a mirror.

OPPOSITE

The pigmented concrete floor and steps, which stay cool even in summer, lead

down into the master bedroom, where French doors open onto the back garden.

A bathing platform with a sunken bath forms the bedhead.

ABOVE

An old galvanised-iron bucket catches the drips from the shower. Behind, colourful geraniums and hibiscus spill from white-rendered planter boxes, while hot-pink Mandevilla is being trained to grow along wires attached to the paling fence.

OPPOSITE

A flight of stairs, with a different style of balustrade on either side, links the upper deck with the back garden. The outdoor shower is used on returning from the nearby beach. Woven wooden roller blinds hung from the underside of the deck are pulled down in order to keep the master bedroom cool in summer.

SET IN STONE

· [MIDDLE HARBOUR]

What is generally thought to constitute good architecture in Australia these days is that which responds to both the climate and the landscape. But it took a couple of overseas-born and-trained architects to first attempt to respond to the native bush. American Walter Burley Griffin moved to Australia in 1914 with his wife Marion Mahony, having won an international competition to set out and design Canberra, Australia's new capital city. Sadly, like Jørn Utzon — the Danish architect who many years later won an international competition to design the Sydney Opera House — Griffin suffered the ignominy of seeing his vision stunted by small-minded bureaucrats, and six years later he resigned from the project.

By that time, however, he and Mahony had established practices in both Sydney and Melbourne and were working on a range of other projects. One — the Greater Sydney Development Association — involved the purchase of spectacular sandstone escarpment land in the northern suburb of Castlecrag, overlooking the serene waters of Middle Harbour.

Griffin and Mahony's vision for the suburb — a community of residential buildings that responded to the environment — was way ahead of its time. There were to be no boundaries, with pathways meandering through the bush. Each house was to be built of local sandstone or the Knitlock system of concrete blocks (Griffin's own invention), which resembled stone. The architecture and interior details were to echo the topography, colours and forms of the surrounding native bushland. Even the houses' flat roofs were to be made into roof gardens, so, when viewed from above, they would be virtually indistinguishable from the surrounding vegetation.

Despite lending authorities being unimpressed by the experimental nature of the houses and refusing to lend money to prospective buyers, the Castlecrag community grew, attracting like-minded, environmentally conscious residents, who were considered at the time to be very bohemian.

The Fishwick house, built in 1929 for the substantial sum of £3000, is the largest, most innovative and intact of the fourteen houses that remain today. Its significance at both state and national levels is recognised by its listing with the National Trust of Australia and its recent registration on the National Estate.

Although the block on which the house is built is wedge-shaped and falls away steeply, its position (just below the highest point on the peninsula) and easterly aspect made it the most sought-after block on the estate. To capture the view of Middle Harbour, the two-storey house was built at the top of the block which, at just seven metres wide, is its narrowest point. The influence of Frank Lloyd Wright, for whom both Griffin and Mahony had worked, is evident in the use of strong horizontal lines. Despite the softening effect of the curved window of the guest bedroom (originally the maids' quarters) at the front of the house, the building appears fortress-like.

Inside, sturdy but elegant tuck-pointed stone walls, washed with golden light from amber-glass skylights, endow the house with a strong, muscular presence. The current owners — who have spent more than two years restoring the house to its original splendour — speak of its inherent vigour and power, which makes it impossible to superimpose their personalities on the building. It remains, in essence, Griffin's ode to the Australian bush.

OPPOSITE
The Fishwick house is constructed of local sandstone and sits at the top of its terraced, wedge-shaped block. When the current owners bought the house, the gardens were quite wild. As dense undergrowth was cleared, some of the original garden paths were uncovered and restored.

BELOW
The upstairs deck affords breathtaking views over the bushland to Middle Harbour, with a glimpse of the ocean in the distance.

ABOVE RIGHT & LEFT

Entry to the house is via a narrow passageway, past twenty-five tall, mirror-backed amber glass panels. The angle of the glazing bars over the front-door glass is echoed in the Y-shaped glazing bars over all the external first-floor windows and doors. Once inside, visitors are drawn to one of the house's unique features – an arched, fixed window piercing the chimney breast in the living room on the other side of the wall, which allows a framed view of of the vista beyond the house.

LEFT

The dining-room ceiling originally featured twin fish tanks, which acted as unusual skylights. These were removed in the 1930s and replaced with convential skylights, fitted with amber cathedral glass. During renovations, most of the original rimu floorboards were retained – laid directly onto a mixture of sand, cement and bitumen to repel termites, alleviate moisture and regulate the temperature inside.

ABOVE

Inside the entrance vestibule, massive concrete pillars frame sets of French doors,

leading into the dining room on one side and the library on the other. The pillars,

mottled with olive-green, bronze and gold paint, resemble a forest of tree trunks.

RIGHT

The library was not included in the original plan, and Griffin had to excavate

below the main bedroom to create space. The room is painted in the same warm

red as that used to pick out the external windows and doors.

RIGHT, FROM TOP TO BOTTOM

A ceiling-mounted light in the study
is a replica of one designed by Walter
Burley Griffin for his first speculative
house on the estate. The tiled fireplace
in the second bedroom is another of
four fireplaces in the house; each is
different in design and character.
The table lamp in the living room is a
reproduction of the ceiling light in the
study (but turned upside down).

OPPOSITE

The focal point of the living room is
the fireplace, with its divided flue and
fixed, arched window that pierces
the chimney breast. From the entrance
vestibule on the other side of the
chimney, this window frames a view
of the garden and harbour in the
distance. Bulkheads flanking the
fireplace conceal uplighting, adding to
the sense of an airy, light-filled room.

ABOVE

The upstairs hallway is lit by an unusual, geometrically shaped skylight.

The ceiling is deliberately low, to emphasise the change of height in each of the

three bedrooms. This device was used by the architect in many areas of the house.

LEFT

In the master bedroom, the bed faces seven windows, with Y-shaped glazing bars.

These create an arc, which is aligned through 180 degrees to catch northern

sunlight throughout the day as it filters through the surrounding trees.

ECLECTIC MOOD

· [EASTERN SUBURBS]

ABOVE

View from the balcony of the nearby Vaucluse amateur sailing club, framed by the trunk of a huge Norfolk Island pine. Beyond, boats are moored in Watson's Bay.

OPPOSITE

At one end of the terrace, two slatted French bistro chairs are arranged around a wire table. An old French park bench sits against the wall.

Annie Emms believes it was fate that led her to this house in Vaucluse, one of Sydney's prestigious eastern harbourside suburbs. Restoring old houses and furniture used to be her creative outlet, but since moving to this house — which many years before was lived in by another artist — her creativity has blossomed, and seven years ago Emms herself began to paint.

Her vibrant, colourful canvases now hang in every room of the house; even the bathrooms are adorned with her exuberant oils. The paintings define the mood of the house, which is energetic and mentally stimulating. Emms firmly believes that a combination of the generous size of the rooms, the various levels and the artwork has a positive effect on all who enter. Children in particular respond to the colourful artwork, as well as the eclectic mix of furnishings and objects.

The way the house has been able to change and grow as Emms' family has grown is another feature that pleases her. She refers to it as the protean factor. But the house's changing form probably says more about her own ability to be flexible and generous than any mystical architectural quality. On first moving in, fifteen years ago, she divided the house into three separate, self-contained apartments, which enabled Annie and her husband to share it harmoniously with her two teenage sons from a previous marriage.

As the boys grew up and moved out, temporary and also permanent walls were removed, enlarging the living area into one generous open-plan space. It leads onto a sun-drenched terrace with views across the harbour to bushy military reserve land on Middle Head.

With the help of Nadia Cohen, an architect with Folk Lichtman (and now a firm friend of

Emms), the long, narrow and very dark kitchen was shifted forward, towards the dining area and the view, enabling a laundry and another bathroom to be slotted in behind it.

The most arresting design element, however, is to be found one level up, in the entrance. Arrived at after a walk through a shady, private forecourt from the front gate, the entrance is visually dominated by a Gaudi-esque cast-iron balustrade that wraps around two short flights of stairs: one, up to two bedrooms and a bathroom; the other, down to the living area. The flamboyant balustrade was the result of a long search to find an artisan whose vision was in sympathy with Emms' own. After meeting with several blacksmiths, she was impressed by Ross Woodcock's inspiring studio surroundings in the Southern Highlands, south of Sydney. She invited him to her house, showed him the entrance hall and then placed her complete trust in his ability to create something perfect. To this day she remains enthralled by the result.

She also enlisted Cohen's help to rearrange the master bedroom, which takes the place of two previous bedrooms, and to make sense of the en-suite bathroom. The master bedroom is now a heavenly, private eyrie, complete with a fireplace and sitting area at one end, and a very feminine sleeping space at the other. French doors open onto two Juliet balconies facing the water.

Steps at the side of the house lead down to a swimming pool and boatshed far below. Beyond is a small, private beach, shared with only a few neighbouring houses. In the near distance, sailboats moored in Watson's Bay bob up and down on the swell. There is no doubt that such a sensuous place will continue to inspire a succession of creative souls.

OPPOSITE & ABOVE

The entrance to the house is dominated by a wrought-iron balustrade, featuring marine plants and flowers, which leads up to the landing and a pair of old French doors (above) to the master bedroom. In the foreground is a large 1920s concrete crucible from India.

LEFT & BELOW

The landing and a carved timber door from South America opposite can be glimpsed through a pair of old French doors, which the owner had fitted to lead into the enlarged master bedroom. Hanging on the side of a Baltic pine wardrobe is an antique silk kimono, which was bought at a country auction. On the left is an old English oak gate-leg table with a vase of gerberas on top – one of the owner's favourite flowers because of their brightly coloured petals.

RIGHT

Behind the sofa at one end of the master bedroom is an old marble-topped European café table. The bed is partly obscured by a length of handmade fabric by Penny Simmons. A Gabbeh rug, dyed with vegetable dyes, adds a jolt of colour to the room. A sybaritic en-suite bathroom and dressing area can be glimpsed leading off the bedroom on the right.

OPPOSITE & ABOVE

The floors and walls of the capacious en-suite bathroom and dressing area are tiled with Vietnamese pigment-dyed concrete tiles in muted yellows and creams, while the top of the vanity unit and the steps up to the bath are clad in Saturnia stone. The ceramic sculpture on the turned wooden plinth to the left was crafted by the owner's son, Tom Schutzinger. The owner cut up the floor and wall tiles to create a mosaic on the pillar that separates the vanity unit from the shower behind.

ABOVE & RIGHT

The main bathroom still retains its original, deep-golden glass tiles and old cast-iron

bath. A painting by the owner propped on the bath taps is called, appropriately,

The Bath. Unattractive white tiles had been used around the shower recess, so the

owner – unable to find any more of the golden tiles – retiled the shower and floor

in a mix of blue, mustard and pale-green tiles. The mosaic-surrounded mirror was

made by a French friend called Alain Cactus. His adopted surname reflects the

second of his two passions.

LEFT & ABOVE

A wall separating the living and dining rooms was removed to unite the space, and the carpeted concrete floors were replaced by the recycled tallowwood floorboards. An oil painting by Melbourne artist Kirka Mora hangs over the fireplace, while below rests a painted tin valance from an old shop. Both the fire screen and the basket were woven from recycled wire by Victorian artists Shades of Gray.A slightly surreal-looking sculpture on a silver tray adorns the top of an old Austrian grain box, while on the recycled oregon dining table sit a sextet of glass candle-holders.

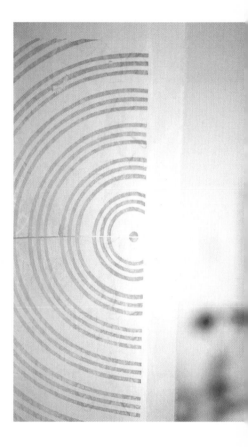

LEFT & ABOVE

The house is an interesting mix of old and new. A large, antique clockface on the wall of the living area was brought back by the owner from a small town in Belgium, where it had been replaced by a neon sign. Beneath it is a Victorian tea caddy with a trio of old English pewter jelly moulds. Hanging on the wall of the study is a hand-painted and -gilded picture frame from South America. The historical religious painting it once framed was deemed by the authorities to be too culturally important to be exported. By contrast, a modern curtain in the master bedroom was commissioned by the owner.

SEA CHANGE

• [NORTHERN PENINSULA]

ABOVE

In the entrance hall a large Spanish mirror with an intricate metal frame hangs above a French sideboard

OPPOSITE

A large, old, French cast-iron candelabra hangs over the dining table. It is attached, via a long chain, to the exposed rafters above the void.

Arriving at this beach house, in an exclusive street on Sydney's northern peninsula, is a slightly confronting but, equally, pulse-racing experience. The dark-green building looks sexy and mysterious. Green was chosen for the exterior to make the house appear smaller than it really is. Through the slatted cedar gates, a large, ribbed terracotta pot can be seen spot lit in the gloom.

Once admitted, the path to the front door is across a low-roofed forecourt paved in granite cobblestones, with a garage on either side. Around one side of the house, pots of bamboo sit in a walled garden bed waiting to be planted. They will soon create a thick green screen, forming one side of a dark corridor (the other, the side of the house) that leads to the front door proper.

One knock and two old and heavy, panelled timber doors creak back on their hinges to reveal the interior. There's an immediate sense of Barragan-meets-Bali: dusty rose pink, roughly rendered walls; wide, polished, hardwood floorboards; exposed rafters; a mix of antique furnishings and exotic objects. The house even smells exotic, courtesy of the linseed oil used to polish the hardwood timber floorboards. All the timber — including the handsomely fissured tallow-wood boards, the massive rafters, the shutters made of dressed hardwood planking, and the weathered internal doors — comes from an old wharf.

Texture is one element that the owner admires of the work of Mexican architect Luis Barragan. She stayed in one of his houses many years ago and the experience was a potent one, remaining with her long after she'd returned home. For years her family had enjoyed

holidays in the old shack that stood on the waterside block, but when she and her husband finally decided to rebuild (needing more room for their growing family), she wanted an organic house with Barragan-like strong, sculptural forms.

She bought the front doors first. The huge, handsome, timber-panelled doors from a convent in Spain provided the tone for the detailing, which was to be rugged and rustic. Architect Walter Barda, who had designed a house further along the beach, was commissioned, and he worked closely with interior designer Michael Love during the initial construction stages. (Thomas Hamel, another interior designer, stepped in later to provide the finishing touches.)

Unlike the owner, Barragan was not the driving inspiration for Barda, although he admits that the house, with its thick walls, has a muscular and sculptural form – qualities often associated with Barragan's work. Rather, it was the symmetry of the plan that determined the design, necessitated by the narrowness of the block (twelve metres wide). This left little room to do anything interesting on either side, so Barda chose to bring light into the house via a two-storey, glass-roofed void in the centre, which reads a little like a classic Roman atrium.

The edges of the glass roof frame the sky, and another small, square window at the back of the first floor frames a view (seen from the sitting room) of the wooded hill behind the house. For Barda, the house works almost like a large version of an old-fashioned box camera: its pinhole view of the hill links the house by the water to the native, bushy landscape behind, while the main windows at the front act like the lens, drawing in the larger view.

OPPOSITE

The architect chose to step the house back, like a wedding cake, to reduce its bulk and visual impact from the beach. The local council were so pleased with the architect's sensitivity that it based all future planning and building codes on the house.

BELOW

Greenery surrounds the house, and cacti grow in a planter boxes outside the master bedroom and bathroom.

RIGHT

A French oak buffet near the dining area holds linen, china and glassware.

Sandstone treads cap the steps leading to the first floor. A large African fertility

symbol carved in timber stands in a niche opposite the dining table.

ABOVE

A cobblestone path around the side of the house leads to a pair of heavy, panelled

timber front doors, which were originally from a Spanish convent. They both have

openable sections – a precursor to today's spyhole. The owners bought the doors

first, deciding they were rather pretty, and then had the house built around them.

OPPOSITE, LEFT & BELOW

This shot of the first-floor mezzanine reveals the monumental quality of the architecture. Massive recycled timber rafters support a glass roof that acts like a giant skylight. The heavy iron chain hanging from them supports a candelabra, which hangs over the dining table directly below. A seventeenth-century Spanish metal mirror hangs at the end of the upstairs hallway, framed by the walls of the bedrooms on either side.

ABOVE & RIGHT

The reproduction gilded mirror hanging on the chimney breast in the sitting area was chosen for its irregular shape, which provides a nice contrast with the two square still-life paintings hanging on either side. French Provincial sideboards flanking the fireplace are used to store video and hi-fi equipment. An Italian silver gilt stool, upholstered in a kilim, sits in front of the fireplace. Each of the children's rooms are split level with a sitting room above the sleeping area. The cast-iron firedogs, produced locally, have an Australian flavour: one is a kangaroo; the other, an emu.

OPPOSITE

Folding glass doors at one end of the sitting room mean that it can be opened up completely to the deck outside. A fragrant murraya hedge defines the side boundary of the property, and a trio of palms adds a tropical touch to the view of Pittwater. The house is called Bukutilla – Aboriginal for 'quiet place by the water'.

BELOW LEFT & RIGHT

A row of palm trees under-planted with ivy lines the southern side of the house, reinforcing the sense of seclusion within its boundaries. Banquettes set at right angles on either side of the rear deck provide permanent seating for meals or just relaxing. A lantern sits on the cedar table, in readiness for night-time gatherings.

RIGHT & ABOVE

An Aubusson tapestry hangs above a Spanish table standing
against the wall in the dining area. On either side is a
pair of seventeenth-century Dutch brass wall sconces which
illuminate dinner parties. A trio of blue-and-white Chinese
lidded jars, bought in Hong Kong, add a splash of colour to
the room. Wood features strongly throughout the open-plan
living area. Built-in sideboards, beneath the plate racks in
the kitchen, were constructed using recycled timber.

OPPOSITE

Plate racks built over the windows on either side of the double Zanussi oven are an interesting way of disguising the view of the neighbouring house. A rustic timber table and bench seats provide a casual seating area.

BELOW

The architect, Walter Barda, designed the door fixtures around the house. An attractively simple T-shaped piece of timber slides back and forth inside a recess to open and close the door.

RIGHT & ABOVE

The bath in the en-suite to the master bedroom is encased in rounded plaster that
has been painted white. There are no wall tiles to interrupt the smooth lines of the
rendered walls. Beside the bath is a wooden-shuttered window overlooking a
cacti-filled planter box at one end of the private terrace, and the bay beyond. On
the window sill stands a matching pair of silver-topped glass bottles.

THE HIGH LIFE

· [INNER EAST]

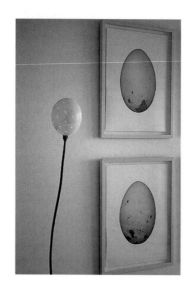

ABOVE

A lamp made from a pierced ostrich egg echoes the subject matter of the paintings hanging in the bedroom.

OPPOSITE

An old French bookcase at one end of the kitchen is filled with a collection of white Pillivuyt china and cream-ware. The streamlined galley kitchen is just large enough to accommodate a marble-topped breakfast table and two slipcovered, spoon-backed chairs.

The owners of this apartment, which is situated in an Art Deco building in Potts Point, enjoy the kind of life to which many people aspire: a chic city pied-à-terre and a cottage in the country. It's the yin and yang required to survive in the modern world – the stresses of living and working in a big metropolis need to be balanced by the calm serenity of a weekend retreat.

It was almost a decade ago when owners Grant Douglas and John Gilbert recognised their mutual desire to flee the city on weekends. At the time they were living in a substantial terrace in the inner-city suburb of Redfern. They searched for months for their ideal retreat, staying everywhere within a two-hour radius of Sydney, but it wasn't until a couple of years later that they eventually found and bought a small but charming 1920s weatherboard cottage in the Blue Mountains, about two and a half hours' west of Sydney.

From the very first weekend they spent there, they were hooked, and their glamorous town house quickly became redundant. There was nothing for it but to sell the city house and find a smaller apartment. The day their house sold, they found a one-bedroom apartment with water views in The Macleay Regis – one of Sydney's grand 1930s apartment buildings in a leafy boule-vard in the inner city – which was available for rent. They snapped it up and, some time later, when the owner wanted to sell, they bought it. Their living arrangements were finally complete.

While their country house takes in a breathtaking view west over bush to a green valley bordered by distant blue hills, the apartment faces another equally panoramic sweep east across Sydney Harbour. And it's a view that's enjoyed from every room — including the bathroom.

The feeling inside the apartment is chic and elegant. After the serious stone-clad walls of the handsome entrance foyer downstairs, as well as the corridors leading to the apartment, the mood is lightened on entering, both by the view and the monochromatic colour scheme. Off-white walls are broken only by the windows, which are clad in timber Venetian blinds painted a slightly darker shade. Crisp, white, slipcovered upholstery is balanced by seriously dark timbers, and the original cypress pine parquet floor grounds the rooms. The effect of various shades of white creates a calm, understated environment that lets the view sing.

The Art Deco origins of the heritage-listed building are obvious. Apart from the parquet floor, the generous proportions of the rooms, the high ceilings and the cornices, the en-suite bathroom is still lined with its original tiles and the balcony edge remains defined by an elegant curved steel railing.

The provenance of furniture and objects that fill the one-bedroom apartment — a Philippe Starck dining table and day bed, a 1930s walnut coffee table, Lalique glass, and groupings of the sensuous ceramics of local artist Gwyn Hanssen Pigott — sound a tasteful note, and at night the apartment sparkles with elegant sophistication. Although the owners do most of their entertaining in the country, inviting guests up for the weekend, groups of friends often gather at the apartment for drinks before dining in one of the area's many local restaurants.

The apartment is more formal than the country house, which suits the pace of city life – however, both places feel like home, or rather, the east wing and the west wing of the one home.

OPPOSITE & BELOW

The apartment enjoys spectacular views over the harbour, across Elizabeth Bay to Clarke Island and out to the heads. Pots of bromeliads ring the edge of the small curved balcony. Two slatted chairs and a café table provide a ringside vantage point. (And, when the owners are out, Fifi the cat has the view to herself.)

RIGHT & BELOW

The white canvas slipcovers transform the furniture, emphasising its sculptural

forms, which, in turn, pick up on the simple, Zen-like shapes of collected objects,

including a cast-resin copy of a Cycladic head, bought at the Louvre. The use of

varying shades of off-white throughout the apartment adds a textural element,

with the layers of different hues providing a palette of subtle depth. Above a

fruitwood daybed are three collagraphs by Fabienne Artaud. An Australian 1930s

walnut-veneer coffee table holds books and a Phalaneopsis *orchid.*

ABOVE

At the far end of the living room, two tub chairs are covered
in crisp, white canvas slipcovers. In front of them is an African
washing stool. Behind, on the sideboard, is a delicate sculpture
by Mike van Niekirk that is made of naturally shed porcupine
quills collected on Table Mountain in South Africa.

OPPOSITE

An intimate dining area and small balcony lead off the living
room. The day bed, dining table and a pendant light hanging
over it are by Philippe Starck. Three ceramic vessels by
Australian potter Gwyn Hanssen Pigott are displayed on top
of a 1940s Swedish cabinet that houses the television.

LEFT & ABOVE

Fifi the cat reclines on antique pure linen bed sheets in the apartment's bedroom.

Behind the bed is a Swedish bookcase that serves as a bedhead. The series of nine

egg drawings in a symmetrical grid on the wall are by Jonathan Delafield-Cook.

The Ostrich egg standard lamp is by Sydney-based designer Mike van Niekirk.

RIVERSIDE RETREAT

• [LANE COVE RIVER]

ABOVE & OPPOSITE

The impressive entrance foyer is a two-storey-high void, lined with limestone. An elaborately sculpted wrought-iron balustrade leads the eye upwards. The floor of the foyer is tiled in antiquated marble, which has been continued through into the family room and kitchen. Hanging above a Louis XV commode against one wall is a gilt-framed Louis XVI mirror.

The Sydney Harbour foreshore is long and meandering, but it's also very varied. For a start, there's a northern side and a southern side. The southern, city side, faces north and is bathed in sun for most of the day, while the northern side is swathed in shadows. Small sandy beaches, exposed rockpools and huge golden sandstone boulders perched right at the water's edge are found both north and south. There are bustling working areas with creaking timber wharves, yacht-filled bays and sheltered coves. Sometimes what's referred to as the harbour isn't really the harbour at all, but the green and glassy waters of rivers or creeks that run into it.

This gracious residence enjoys a wide water-frontage of over thirty metres, facing north across Lane Cove River, to the west of the Harbour Bridge. It's a totally different view to those enjoyed by waterfront houses in the eastern suburbs, which tend to be more expansive, looking across stretches of navy-blue water to the distant lower north shore.

Here the view — all 180 degrees of it — is much more intimate. The water is calmer. Yachts bob lazily at their moorings and sleek cruisers are tied up to innumerable jetties that poke their long, thin fingers into the quiet waters of the river.

It is a serene sight, especially from the lawn in front of the house. Split into two levels, the lower area is home to the swimming pool and a large Port Jackson fig, a species native to Sydney. At night, uplights embedded in the turf highlight the tree's sculptural form, making a striking statement against the inky blackness of the water which can be appreciated from nearly every room in the house.

The word 'house' is really a misnomer for a residence as imposing as this. Its architect, Michael Suttor, refers to it as a villa — which feels more apt. There are certainly many classical elements in its architecture, such as the colonnaded façade, the summer loggia, vaulted ceilings, marble-clad floors and an impressive sweeping stone staircase with a hand-wrought metal balustrade. The antique furnishings and refined decor are also suitably classical in temperament — the signature style of interior designer Michael Love, who worked closely with Suttor.

The ground floor is book-ended by formal rooms: a drawing room facing east and a dining room, looking west, opening onto a sheltered loggia that's just right for summer lunches. Between these two rooms is the family domain: a generous, open-plan living, dining and kitchen area with floor-to-ceiling glazed doors along its northern wall that open directly onto the front lawn. A small wing off the kitchen provides a preparation area that's tucked out of view. Directly across the hallway is a butler's pantry, which is used when the owners entertain on a grand scale.

Upstairs are the bedrooms. The capacious master suite — with a bedroom and sitting area, a separate dressing room, an en-suite bathroom and its own private terrace — is playfully referred to by the owner as 'the apartment'. He jokes that, when his two young daughters become teenagers, he and his wife will retreat to their 'apartment', giving them the run of the house.

With all its classical features, this house-cum-villa feels as though it has been there for decades, but it has only recently replaced a smaller 1950s bungalow, which did not take full advantage of the site – and such a splendid site deserves an equally fine residence.

OPPOSITE & ABOVE

The grounds in front of the house are split into two terraces. On the upper terrace is a lawn fringed with hedging; on the lower, a handsome Port Jackson fig and an azure-blue swimming pool. The colour of the water is repeated in the shaggy blue flower heads of agapanthus. Hidden underneath the lawn, behind the swimming pool, is a large play and storage room.

ABOVE & RIGHT

From the end of the jetty – the house, with its colonnaded façade
– has a handsome, gracious air. Shading the upstairs terrace is
a trio of canvas awnings. Beside the timber jetty sits a painted
boathouse, and over the rocky shoreline, to its left, spills a froth
of brilliant scarlet bougainvilleas and agapanthus blooms.

RIGHT

The Italian limestone fireplace in the family sitting room was designed by Michael Suttor, the architect. To absorb some of the noise bouncing off all the hard surfaces in the room, interior designer Michael Love decided to line the ceiling with upholstered panels. The north-facing windows are clad in wide-bladed timber Venetian blinds, which are fully automated to cut the heat and glare.

BELOW

A 1720s chair sits in the entrance foyer beneath a French chandelier wall light. The lights were chosen for their elongated form and the welcoming glow they cast at night. The drawing room can be seen through an open door directly ahead.

LEFT & ABOVE

The drawing room is used for formal entertaining.
Its walls have been cleverly divided into panels with
simple timber moulding, which gives them both form
and interest. A view of the water is framed by the curtains,
and silhouetted against the window is a German chair,
made in approximately 1730.

ABOVE LEFT & RIGHT

In the formal dining room a nineteenth-century French gilt chandelier hangs over an Italian walnut dining table. The dining chairs, with ebony-stained legs, are upholstered in black fabric. The low bookcase against the far wall is Italian and a herringbone seagrass mat covers the floor.

RIGHT

The curtain fabric and sofa upholstery was hand-printed in Texas, while the two-tone block fringe trimming on both the curtains and ottoman was woven to match in London. Hanging above the nineteenth-century French, red marble fireplace is an eighteenth-century French mirror.

ABOVE

The double stainless-steel industrial oven and worktop in the kitchen is housed
in an alcove, which also conceals a powerful exhaust fan. A large ceramic sculpture
resembling a shard of blue-and-white china sits on top of a plate-drying rack
between two tall cupboards in the service wing of the kitchen.

RIGHT

An Italian walnut dining table, surrounded by reproduction dining chairs covered
with plain canvas slipcovers, is used for casual meals. The walls of the kitchen
and adjacent family room have been finished in mellow gold stucco lucido, a
polished plaster finish.

City

Residences

LIVING COLOUR

• [WOOLLAHRA]

ABOVE

The rear, north-facing courtyard brims over with lush, green vegetation and vibrant blooms.

OPPOSITE

A new staircase with a timber balustrade was built at the end of the central hallway to link all three floors. The walls are lined with paintings from the owners' collection of contemporary Australian art.

T his Victorian, sandstone, semi-detached house epitomises gracious living, demonstrating just how well an old house can be restored and reinvigorated in the process. There is nothing quaint about this restoration — not a reproduction pedestal basin or brass light-fitting in sight. Instead the house — both inside and out — has been carefully repaired and renewed, with a seamless transition from the traditional rooms at the front to the modern additions at the rear.

However, the house's well-groomed appearance hides a colourful past. According to Louise Bell of Interni (who, with her business partner Madeline Lester, designed and oversaw the renovations), it has been many things to many people – including, at one stage, a brothel. When the current owners bought the house, it had been divided into three dilapidated flats.

Its chequered history meant that very little original fabric remained. But despite its sorry condition the house still had a sense of soul, which is what the owners immediately responded to. Its age (circa 1867) and its position — in an elegant, heritage-listed thoroughfare in the eastern suburbs of Sydney — meant that the handsome façade had to be retained. The badly slumped verandah was rebuilt and retiled using tessellated tiles fired to match the originals. Old cast-iron lace was found to replace the missing valance, and the balustrade was repaired.

While the exterior was attended to, Lester and Bell began to make sense of the odd layout and disparately proportioned rooms inside. As the owners like to entertain on a grand scale, one major requirement was for generous entertaining areas. The two large rooms to the right of the entrance hall became the formal living and dining rooms, while on the other side of the hallway

three smaller rooms were turned into a study, bathroom and child's bedroom. A new staircase was built at the end of the hallway to link all three floors, replacing two separate staircases.

Tacked onto one corner of the rear of the house, a three-storey tower, which the local council deemed worthy of retention and which had housed three bathrooms (one on each level for each flat), was rebuilt and re-clad with weatherboards. Its top floor is now an en-suite bathroom for the guest bedroom, while its middle floor contains a butler's pantry that leads off the dining room. On the lower level, the space is used as a small sunroom beside the casual eating area.

The large master bedroom on the first floor was also reconfigured, creating a dressing room and en-suite bathroom. The lower ground floor is now the heart of the house and comprises a large, well-equipped kitchen with a walk-through pantry, a huge cellar, a small study and a family room opening directly onto the north-facing courtyard garden.

Throughout the house the repetition of materials adds to the strength of the design, which is reinforced by the high quality of finishes. The clean classicism of honed Carrara marble features in all of the bathrooms, as well as the kitchen and butler's pantry. Brass mesh-fronted cupboards hide heating outlets and provide storage in the front rooms, master bedroom and family room.

The owners' decision to begin collecting Australian art coincided with buying the house, so Lester and Bell had to make sure that there would be enough hanging space. Both the house and art collection were, therefore, simultaneous works-in-progress. The house is long since complete but the art collection continues to grow, filling the house with colour and energy.

OPPOSITE

Glimpsed through an iron palisade fence, the elegant nineteenth-century house has a distinctly colonial feel to it. Its handsome stone façade, with its restored cast-iron valance and balustrade, has been returned to its former glory, belying the modern and comfortable interior that has been created by the owners.

LEFT & ABOVE

Bi-fold glazed doors on one side of the family room enable it to be opened to
the courtyard garden. The idea of indoors and outdoors merging into one space is
reinforced by the use of pale flagstones, which pave the family-room floor and
the courtyard. Pieces of antique furniture and a Persian rug are balanced by the
modern artwork, hand-crafted objects and tribal sculptures that sit on top of
built-in cupboards housing hi-fi and video equipment.

FAR LEFT & LEFT

The formal living and dining rooms retain their original floorboards, which have been stained to darken their natural colour. A soft ochre was chosen for the walls, to complement the owners' collection of modern Australian art. In both rooms, built-in bookshelves fill in the narrower of the alcoves on one side of the chimney breast. Circular-design rattan dining chairs complement the dark-wood table.

ABOVE

As the owners often entertain on a grand scale, the kitchen has to function as
a family eat-in kitchen but also be able to cope when catering for large numbers.
It is given a classic, yet functional feel with Carrara marble splashbacks,
stainless-steel worktops and a large island bench topped with recycled timber.

LEFT

The lower ground floor is the heart of the house, with the kitchen the centre of
activity. Here a large, old timber table with chairs and a wooden settle provides
a casual eating area. The light and airy family room leads off to one side,
effectively enclosing the rear courtyard.

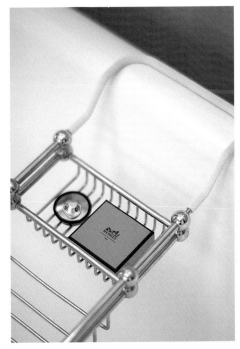

OPPOSITE & ABOVE

The owners insisted that the marble tiles cladding the floors and walls of their
en-suite bathroom stop at dado height to allow for extra hanging space for their
ever-expanding art collection. The freestanding bath rests on custom-made timber
cradle supports. The opaque shower blind at the back of the double shower can be
raised to reveal French doors leading onto a rear sun-drenched balcony. A row of
glass shelves holding perfume bottles is reflected in the mirror, further accentuating
the sense of symmetry and order.

ABOVE, RIGHT & OPPOSITE

The large master bedroom on the first floor was totally reconfigured. The bed
is positioned in the centre of the room, facing the fireplace over which hangs
a painting by artist John Olsen. Two Hang Dynasty ceramic figures stand on the
marble mantelpiece. The freestanding bedhead, with storage space on both sides,
creates a natural walkway to the wardrobes and dressing area behind. All the
joinery is given a period feel with woven brass-mesh cupboard fronts.

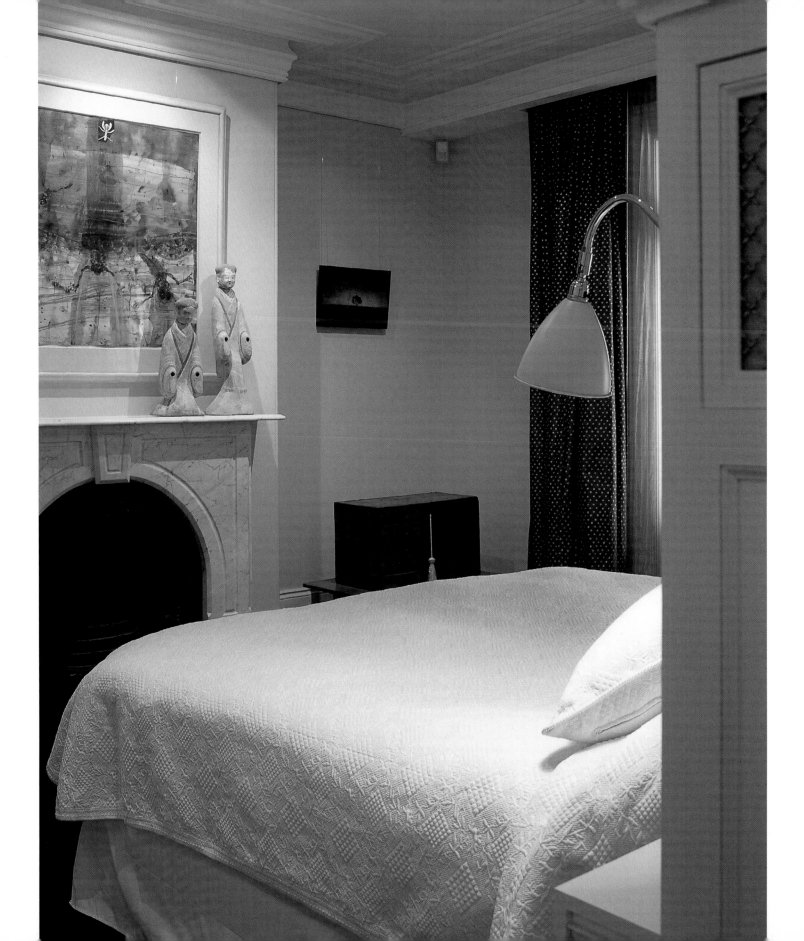

INDUSTRIAL CHIC

· [INNER CITY]

ABOVE

Viewed from the outside, the new walls of plywood, corrugated metal and concrete rise up from behind the masonry walls of the old warehouse.

OPPOSITE

The rooftop of the timber-clad studio beside the house is enclosed with a high, sloping balustrade of cedar battens, creating an ideal outdoor barbecue and sunbathing area.

It's a mixed architectural metaphor, but this contemporary, urban 'farm shed' works. Its rationale is simple. The owner grew up in the country, and has a fondness for both the materials and inherent characteristics of farm buildings. He recalls that whenever a visitor arrived at the farmhouse looking for someone, he or she would be told to go down to the shed. The shed was always the centre of activity, and there you'd be sure to find the person you were looking for.

Stephen Grant now lives in an environment that's as urban as they come, but a few years ago he bought his own city 'shed' — a 1920s single-storey building with brick walls and a corrugated-iron roof. Built originally to house an ironmonger's business, it was later used as a timber storage depot before being left empty and near-derelict.

After Grant bought it, he asked architect Graham Jahn to transform it into a house with 'a shed-like feel' because of the architect's reputation for working with old industrial buildings, retaining both their history and integrity.

The first glimpse of the building, at the end of a lane, is immediately intriguing. Rising up from behind the old brick walls is an angled line of plywood panels and then another of corrugated metal crowning the building. It's a vibrant mix of textures and materials: new with old, rough against smooth. The original ground-floor windows are filled with translucent glass, denying the passer-by even the tiniest glimpse of the interior.

The entrance — a blank metal door with a buzzer beside it — is around the corner, on the third of three narrow inner-city laneways that mark the boundaries of the building. The door

opens into a roofed portico and a set of travertine-edged concrete steps lead down from the portico to a paved, north-facing courtyard with a large lily pond. The new dwelling rears up on the right. On top is a box, clad in shiny corrugated metal, containing the master bedroom and en-suite bathroom. Below that is the living area — a generously large living and dining space, with a kitchen at one end. Sliding glass doors along the northern face of the floor open onto a balcony overlooking the courtyard. On the ground floor — behind an intricate, louvred screen of hexagonal aluminium panels — are two more bedrooms, a bathroom, laundry and an office, with two garages tucked behind.

Accessible from this level, or via stepping stones across the lily pond, is another room that juts out at an angle into the courtyard, its walls clad with ribbed cedar battens. At present it's filled with Grant's son's musical equipment, but it has no set purpose. A meditation room, art studio, music room — it's whatever it needs to be at the time, while, above, its rooftop deck (accessed directly from the kitchen) provides a sheltered place for barbecues and outdoor dining.

Standing in the portico it's obvious that the new building has been slid neatly inside the perimeter walls of the old – the interior face of the wall that encloses one side of the courtyard is battle-scarred, with holes where the original rafters were once slotted, and marks where steps led up to a mezzanine floor. However, retaining the perimeter walls of the original building has respected the streetscape, while allowing a private, inward-looking sanctuary to be created inside: an open house that's always full of people, just like the country shed of Grant's childhood.

ABOVE

A stone statue of Buddha bought in Vietnam sits on a plinth under the portico, just inside the front door.

OPPOSITE

A potted magnolia adds a splash of greenery to the courtyard. Beside it sits a cairn of river-worn rocks, assembled by the owner. The ribbed cedar battens of the music room — also used as meditation space — contrast texturally with the various materials of the main house.

OPPOSITE & BELOW

The house contains a wonderful array of textures and materials. In the entrance
stairway, sunlight filters through louvres over the glass roof, creating linear shadow
patterns on the wall. Night, a painting by British artist John Hoyland, dominates the
area. In the courtyard the rough aggregate pavers are contrasted against the pebble-filled
lily pond and a smooth, incised concrete wall. In the living area, the same wall works well
with the exposed timber trusses that held up the roof of the original warehouse.

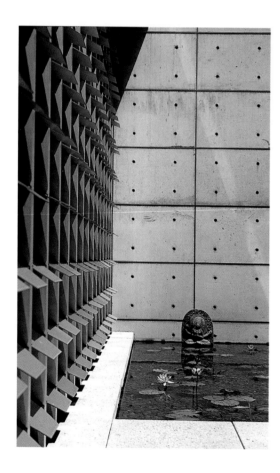

LEFT & BELOW

The kitchen is tucked away at one end of the living space, behind the dining area. It is fitted out with Australian silky oak cupboards and stainless-steel appliances. On the other side of the room, a steel beam used to support the old timber roof trusses has been painted in a strong canary yellow. A series of thirteen acrylics by Guan Wei, called **The Last Supper**, is arranged on the wall from floor to ceiling.

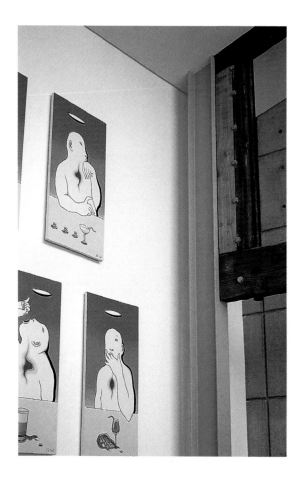

RIGHT

A large, predominantly red canvas by Paco Perez-Valencia hangs above the living
space. Sliding glass doors along the northern side open onto a balcony that
overlooks the courtyard, providing access to the rooftop deck of the adjacent studio.

BELOW

A large oil painting called The Summer's Day, by Australian artist Fred Cress,
dominates the dining area. The timber skirting boards throughout the room are
recessed into the walls, allowing furniture to be butted up directly against them.
The small oil on the floor is by Kumari Mahappen and the heads sitting on the
dining table, fashioned from video cassette tape, are by Fiona Hall.

ABOVE

Architect Graham Jahn enjoys recycling materials on site. Here, timber beams
salvaged from the original building support the roof.

RIGHT

Much of the roof is glazed, filling the interior with suffused light. B & B Italia sofas
stand on a Persian rug, with an Aboriginal pole by Djutjadjuta Mununggur,
Danbarr, dominating the room beside them. The large canvas entitled Sarajevo
hanging in the landing behind is by the Spanish artist Paco Perez-Valencia.

FAR LEFT

A feature of the master bedroom is the framed sheet of glass that provides views into the en-suite bathroom. The shower is totally enclosed – acting like a Turkish bath – and lit from above by a vented skylight.

TOP LEFT

The bathroom cabinetry is clad in American oak. Propped against the mirror is a small abstract landscape painting by Louic Le Groumellec.

BOTTOM LEFT

In the bedroom the bed is pulled away from the wall, allowing breathing space for an oil by Nicholas Harding. On the top of the bed head are some ceramics and a small Thai Buddha sitting in a pool of beads.

GOTHIC GRANDEUR

· [BELLEVUE HILL]

There is a cartouche on one wall of the enclosed courtyard of this two-storey, creeper-clad sandstone house which reads: 'Rona, AEDIF [built] 1883, REFECT [remade] 1951'. What was no doubt erected with some degree of pride is now simply a sad reminder of the fact that this once-intact building was considerably remodelled fifty years ago to create two separate apartments. The enclosed courtyard where the cartouche hangs was originally a grand entrance hall with exposed timber rafters and a first-floor gallery, leading off to the bedrooms. The exquisite timber joinery of the staircase, panelled dado and balustrade have all vanished and the flagstone-paved space is now open to the heavens.

The removal of the hall's steeply pitched roof has affected the exterior appearance of the house as well. Viewed from the rear, the taller middle gable is missing; just the truncated wall beneath it remains. However, all is not lost. Because of its size and location, the building was well documented and the new owners are gradually restoring it to its original splendour.

The Victorian Gothic house was designed by G.A. Morrell, the architect of another grand mansion called Swifts in nearby Darling Point, which is also currently undergoing extensive restoration after being saved from demolition. Rona (the house was named after a small island between Skye and Scotland) was built for Edward Knox, founder of the Colonial Sugar Refineries, a self-made man who chose the land because of its sweeping views down the hill to Double Bay and across the harbour. Although the expanse of the property is now greatly reduced, the current owner has managed to turn the tide slightly. He has bought back an adjacent block

on which to build a lawn tennis court, as well as a charming sandstone house on the boundary that was originally the stables and now serves as guest accommodation. Purchasing this house has also allowed for the continuation of a gravel driveway, or carriage loop, from one side of the property past the back of the house to the far boundary. The grounds have been extensively landscaped with mature trees and shrubs to assume a park-like appearance, with pockets of lush rainforest vegetation and huge, heritage-listed kauri and Norfolk Island pines planted by Knox.

Returning to the house, the current owner — with the help of interior designer Thomas Hamel — has begun restoring the main rooms on the ground floor. The magnificent coffered kauri ceilings have been uncovered, and their soft, honey-coloured gleam now matches that of the high skirting boards, architraves and doors, all fashioned from the same material.

The configuration of the rooms differs from the original but they are still impressive, replete with handsome Gothic furniture and a magnificent collection of early Australian and Pre-Raphaelite paintings and sculpture. With the assistance of consultants in Europe, America and Australia, the owner's art collection continues to grow. Once a month or more, Hamel and a specialist picture-hanger come to the house to help reorganise artworks and make space for more.

Future plans for the house are constantly changing. At present they include remodelling the west wing (originally the kitchen, which caught fire early last century) to create a two-storey gallery of generous proportions. This will at last provide a grand and sizable entertaining space, which is to be expected in a house of Rona's stature and prominence.

OPPOSITE

The grass tennis court was recently constructed on a newly acquired block of land adjacent to the house. From the rear, the missing middle gable over the entrance hall is obvious.

ABOVE

Instead of leading into a grand gallery as it once did, the front portico, with an antique light fitting and personalised doormat, now leads into an internal courtyard.

RIGHT & BELOW

The sitting room's wallpaper was sourced in New York, chosen after buying

the antique patterned rug, in the same city. A trompe l'oeil artist hand-painted

the frieze between the picture rail and the timber cornice using a pattern from

a Gothic design book. An elaborate, gilt French clock sits on the mantelpiece.

A collection of leather-bound books sits in a bookcase against one wall of the

sitting room. Above the bookcase is a painting by John Spencer-Stanhope.

FAR LEFT

This room, which was originally the schoolroom for the first owner's children, suffered greatly during the last round of renovations, and was turned into a double garage. It is now used as a library and television room. The painting above the fireplace is by French artist Bouguereau.

LEFT

A smaller connecting room upstairs now acts as a gallery. In it hangs an impressively scaled painting by Lord Leighton. It was originally one of a triptych that hung in the artist's own entrance hall.

ABOVE & RIGHT

The gallery room in the west wing of the house is decorated in homage to Sir John

Soane, whose house museum is in London. The painting of an archangel comforting

a naked woman was painted by Watts and presented by the artist to the people

of America. For a while it hung in the White House, but was later deemed to be too

risqué and was sold. It eventually turned up in London, where the present owner

bought it. A collection of sculpture by Barbara Tribe lines the wooden mantelpiece.

ABOVE & OPPOSITE

The view from the dining room along the hallway to the staircase is illuminated by light reflecting in from the internal courtyard. All the doors in the main rooms downstairs are crafted in knotted kauri. Elsewhere they are plain, but generally left unpainted. Deeper colours have been used in some of the rooms to provide a foil for the artworks. On the stairs, a large gilt-framed mirror reflects light from the hall.

LEFT

The owner's collection of sculpture extends outside, too. A bronze snail by Barbara Tribe sits on a table on the terrace, while a replica bust awaits others for tea.

ABOVE

It is easy to understand why the house was sited in its present position by Edward Knox, the original owner, as the views are magnificent from every aspect.
The first step was the acquisition of an empty block of land adjacent to the property, which has become a lawn tennis court. The purchase of a neighbouring house allowed for the reinstatement of the gravel carriage loop.

COTTAGE STUDIO

· [INNER WEST]

ABOVE

The new bathroom extension juts out from the rear metal roof, its louvred windows drawing light and air into the upstairs rooms.

OPPOSITE

The north-facing side wall of the studio was fitted with large steel-framed windows and doors that open onto a pair of small decks (one concrete, the other timber), linking the bathhouse with the main building.

One can tell a great deal about an owner's personality from the house they live in. Rosemary Luker's house is a confident amalgam of styles and influences that reveals the many talents of its owner. Although it's unlikely that anyone visiting her house for the first time would be able to guess the fact that Luker has degrees in Psychology and Economics, listening to her entertaining stories you may guess (and quite correctly) that she has another degree in Communication and Journalism. However, it's more likely that the casual visitor would immediately recognise the trained eye of an artist — the fourth string to Luker's very fulsome bow.

The house — a double-fronted freestanding cottage built in the 1870s, topped by two unusual barrel-vaulted dormer windows that peep out of the lichen-covered slate roof — is the perfect canvas for Luker's many talents. It was practically derelict when she bought it, but she lived in it for over a year while waiting for plans drawn up by her architect, Virginia Kerridge to be passed by the local council. The house is situated in a busy but leafy street in an inner-city conservation area, and the council were anxious that it should not be altered too drastically.

From the front, there is little sign of any change. It is only when looking along the northern side of the house that a modern extension of modest proportions can be espied at the rear. Little was done to the front of the house downstairs, except to make it sound with new wiring, plumbing and some plasterwork. The two bedrooms on the upper floor had not been inhabited for nearly twenty years, and pigeons were nesting above doors and windows. After the roof and dormer windows were repaired and reglazed, a compact new bathroom was added upstairs that

cantilevers out from the first floor, disrupting the line of the back section of roof (but visible only when viewed from behind). Apart from providing extra bathroom facilities, its sandblasted, louvred windows draw much-needed ventilation into the other upstairs rooms.

Clad in marine ply, the upstairs bathroom matches the one built downstairs — a separate pavillion or bathhouse at the rear of the house, adjacent to the studio (which replaced the old scullery and a laundry). The cladding material chosen for the bathrooms is deliberately modern – industrial, but also lightweight – to allow the new additions to stand apart visually from the rest of the house. For the same reason (as well as to flood the interior with natural light), steel-framed windows and doors rather than timber ones were installed on either side of the studio.

Every room in the house is filled with interesting objects and artwork, all with fascinating stories, which Luker recounts in her soft lilting voice. Many of the pieces have been found at local and overseas markets, or passed down from grandparents and great-grandparents. Collections tend to be organised thematically, although the common thread linking the objects is often a very personal one.

Two Australian characteristics, humour and able resourcefulness, along with Kerridge's disciplined vision, are the other ingredients that have helped to shape this pared-back, elemental house. Luker and her partner, tree surgeon Russell Freeman, are both essentially down-to-earth, practical people, and so (for all its quirky charm) the house has an honest, approachable, yet totally captivating, appeal — just like the woman who owns it.

OPPOSITE & ABOVE
A staircase, with a simple turned newel post, leads upstairs from the dining room. Slatted French café chairs surround the dining table, and stand on a painted chequerboard floor cloth — the owner's copy of the original style of floor coverings found in servants quarters.

OPPOSITE

In the studio, a canvas painted by the owner (after a Fragonard) sits above the workbench awaiting finishing touches. Visiting friends often recline on an old striped chaise longue and talk to the owner while she works.

ABOVE & LEFT

The pair of gilded metal and timber light sconces with Blackamoor hands was found in Amsterdam. In the studio, a large chest of drawers holds pots of paint, brushes and other miscellaneous artists' paraphernalia.

OPPOSITE & BELOW

In the living room, the paint and varnish has been removed from the original carved timber-surround fireplace to expose a plaster finish. On the mantelpiece stands a metal sculpture by Simeon Nelson called Pierced Rose and, next to a statue of St Vincent, two stuffed pheasants found at the local markets echo the subject of the old colonial tapestry behind. On the coffee table is a marble sculpure by the owner's partner, Russell Freeman, while a colourful grid of painted CD covers by Matthew Johnson hangs above the sideboard.

OPPOSITE

A resin-moulded rose sculpture by Gabrielle Courtenay hangs on the wall outside the
kitchen. The cupboards are water gum, with a recycled brushbox worktop, and the walls
are painted with purple distemper, made to an old recipe that includes rabbit glue.

BELOW LEFT & RIGHT

The service area is concentrated on one side of the kitchen, and is flanked by a pantry
and storage cupboards. On the rear verandah, which leads off the studio and kitchen,
a tiled Moroccan table and two canvas chairs are set up for casual meals.

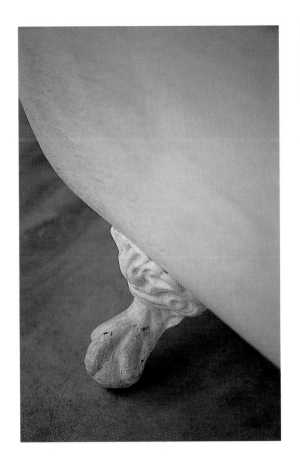

OPPOSITE & LEFT

The cool pale interior of the bathhouse has an almost monastic simplicity. White glass mosaic tiles cover the walls, and the floor is a simple slab of polished concrete. Facing the courtyard garden is a wall of opaque sandblasted glass louvres flanking a steel-framed door. The windows on the northern side let in warm sun. A plaster moulding, some shells and a silver candlestick sit on an old French café table against a wall. Behind is an old faded tapestry, which belonged to the owner's grandmother.

DESIGNER COMFORT

· [EASTERN SUBURBS]

ABOVE

Love's most prized possession, a second-century BC Greek stone relief, stands on its own plinth beside the fireplace in the sitting room.

OPPOSITE

Floor-to-ceiling cupboards line one wall of the dressing room. A Louis XVI marquise is lit by sun streaming through limed plantation shutters.

When interior designer Michael Love first moved into his duplex, he painted the walls a colour he calls Tuscan red. Seven years later, he decided it was time for a change and opted for a sophisticated palette of natural stone balanced by dark charcoal. Bright colour was limited to small flashes of brilliance on various objects and accessories. Eschewing vivid colour in his own surroundings was, Love believes, a natural reaction to working with it all day in the homes of his clients. What he needed was a calm, neutral environment to come home to.

His house is one half of what was originally a 1920s dark-brick block of apartments overlooking a harbourside park and the sparkling waters of Rushcutters Bay to the east of the city. He and a friend bought the three-storey building fourteen years ago and divided it down the middle, converting the four apartments (two on either side) into a pair of spacious city dwellings with the help of architect Susan Rothwell. All that really remains of the original building are the external walls, a pitched tiled roof, and the garages on the ground level.

From the street, the rendered, putty-coloured exterior of the building, with its small eaves and classic proportions, is faintly Georgian. Its elegant façade appears to have influenced the architecture of similar conversions and new houses along the tree-lined boulevard.

Inside, the atmosphere is stately and refined. Every item has been chosen and arranged with an impeccable eye (although Love himself admits that there is more in the house than he would normally suggest for his clients — the inevitable result of a lifetime of collecting). Old Master drawings hang on the walls, and a growing number of treasured antiquities adorn mantel-

pieces and table tops. His favourite period is Louis XVI and much of the furniture dates from this time. But Love is no purist: there are also Regency, Louis XV and modern pieces.

The first floor, which originally housed one two-bedroom apartment, now comprises a spacious double sitting room, with a dining room, kitchen and breakfast area behind it. At one end is a private terrace for sunbathing; at the other, a larger, sheltered terrace for entertaining. Both are linked by a balcony, its front edge defined by a narrow hedge of murraya.

Glazed doors in the dining room lead out onto a paved rear courtyard. Behind stone retaining walls, the garden slopes up steeply towards a fence-line that is hidden by luxuriant foliage. A neat, square swimming pool, tiled in pale turquoise mosaic tiles and fringed with fragrant star jasmine, is reached by climbing a flight of stairs from the courtyard.

Reflections off the water dance on the ceiling above the sisal-covered stone stairs leading to the second floor. Here the original floor plan can be more readily appreciated. The old sun-room is now a dark-hued and chic study, with the original living room transformed into a spacious master bedroom. A dressing room and en-suite bathroom, have taken the place of the original bedrooms and a pale lemon guest bedroom now occupies the space where the kitchen once stood.

The seven-year revamp extended upstairs and the master bedroom was stripped of colour and pattern, its walls reupholstered in a wool-cashmere fabric of the deepest charcoal. It is now the dark, cool, soporific space that Love craves at the end of a hectic day and, despite another seven years having passed, he sees no need to redecorate again – yet.

OPPOSITE

At one end of the kitchen is a breakfast area, which leads to the northern terrace. Around the table are two Louis XVI chairs. The cork floor has been painted with a lattice pattern.

ABOVE

The sheltered rear courtyard, which leads off the dining room, is always cool, so it is the perfect place for outdoor dining. Camellias and mondo grass add to the verdant feel.

RIGHT

Of the four terraces surrounding the
house, the one at the northern end
of the duplex is used most. This is
because it leads off both the kitchen
and living room. Protection is afforded
to its occupants by a timber pergola
that is overlaid with tinted glass.
Lloyd Loom wicker chairs with Indian
cotton cushions are gathered around
a sandstone and iron table.

ABOVE

Standing at either end of timber plantation shutters flanking one side of the
room is a pair of handsome Regency colza lamps on tapering mahogany plinths.
A Directoire lamp sits on a black lacquer Louis XVI console table against one
wall, with an early nineteenth-century French wallpaper panel hanging behind.

RIGHT

The fireplace – its stone mantelpiece adorned with a pair of bronze tazza and
two English bronze-and-gilt candlesticks in the shape of sphinxes – provides a focus
at the northern end of the living room. Above hangs a Regency convex mirror, and
in front stands a Louis XVI stool.

OPPOSITE & BELOW

The walls of the master bedroom are upholstered in a deep, dark charcoal wool and cashmere blend, which the owner chose for its cocooning, soporific effect. To one side, a Regency chair sits in front of an Empire bookcase crowned with a marble bust. A substantial dressing room leads off the bedroom and acts as a walkthrough to the en-suite bathroom (lined with Carrara marble and hand-painted in the Swedish style), in which stands a nineteenth-century French marble bathtub.

SYDNEY GUIDE

• HOTELS

Hotel Inter-Continental
117 Macquarie Street,
Sydney.
Tel: (02) 9253 9000
• *Located in the heart of the
city centre, with views over
the Harbour and Opera House.*

The Kirketon
229 Darlinghurst Road,
Sydney.
Tel: (02) 9332 2011
• *Glamorous restaurant and bar.*

Medusa
267 Darlinghurst Road,
Sydney.
Tel: (02) 9331 1000
• *Designer-decorated, located
in the trendy Kings Cross area.*

The Observatory Hotel
89–113 Kent Street,
Sydney.
Tel: (02) 9256 2222
• *Individually designed rooms
situated in The Rocks.*

Pier One Parkroyal
11 Hickson Road,
Walsh Bay.
Tel: (02) 8298 9999
• *Stylish harbourside setting.*

Regents Court
18 Springfield Avenue,
Potts Point.
Tel: (02) 9358 1533
• *Chic hotel with modernist
furniture collection and a
rooftop garden.*

The Ritz Carlton Double Bay
33 Cross Street,
Double Bay. Sydney
Tel: (02) 9362 4455
• *Luxurious suites with marble
bathrooms. Rooftop sun deck,
pool and fitness centre, all with
harbour views.*

The Russell Hotel
143a George Street,
The Rocks.
Tel: (02) 9241 3543.
• *Built in 1887, with rooftop a
garden overlooking Circular Quay.*

The Regent
199 George Street,
The Rocks.
Tel: (02) 9238 000
• *Historic boutique hotel, situated
minutes from the Opera House.*

W Sydney
6 Cowper Street,
Woolloomoloo.
Tel: (02) 9331 9000
• *Luxurious suites in restored,
heritage Finger Wharf.*

The Westin
1 Martin Place,
Sydney
Tel: (02) 8223 1222
• *Elegance and luxury
in the heart of the city.*

• D I N I N G

Aria
1 Macquarie Street,
East Circular Quay.
Tel: (02) 9252 2555
• *Situated in a building dubbed
'The Toaster' by Sydneysiders.
Fabulous food and luxurious
surrounds.*

The Bathers Pavilion
4 The Esplanade,
Balmoral Beach.
Tel: (02) 9969 2104
• *Fashionable eatery, designed
by Australian architect Alex Popov.*

Bayswater Brasserie
32 Bayswater Road,
Kings Cross.
Tel: (02) 9357 2177
• *Casual restaurant and bar,
where lunch runs into dinner and
on into the small hours. One of
Sydney's institutions.*

Bel Mondo
Level 3,
The Argyle Centre,
12–24 Argyle Street,
The Rocks.
Tel: (02) 9241 3700
• *Fine restaurant in old wool store.*

Forty One
Level 41,
2 Chifley Square,
Sydney.
Tel: (02) 9221 2500
• *Good food and panoramic
views from this restaurant at
the top of the Chifley Tower.*

Mezzaluna
123 Victoria Street,
Potts Point.
Tel: (02) 9357 1988
• *Excellent Italian food with
a view over the city skyline.*

MG Garage
Crown Street,
Surry Hills.
Tel: (02) 9383 9383
• *Voted top restaurant in 1999.*

Quay
Overseas Passenger Terminal,
Circular Quay.
Tel: (02) 9251 5600
• *Wonderful French-inspired
food in elegan, harbourside
surroundings.*

Rockpool
107 George Street,
The Rocks.
Tel: (02) 9252 1888
• *One of Sydney's finest
dining rooms.*

Catalina
Lyne Park,
Rose Bay.
Tel: (02) 9371 0555
• *Modern Australian cusine
in a modern Australian setting.*

• BARS & NIGHTCLUBS

Anti Bar, Bel Mondo
Level 3, The Argyle Centre,
12–24 Argyle Street,
The Rocks.
Tel: (02) 9241 3700
• *Bar serving antipasti.*

Bennelong
Sydney Opera House,
Bennelong Point, Sydney
Tel: (02) 9250 7548
• *Sit in one of Arne Jacobsen's
'Swan' chairs and soak up the
ambience of the famous building
while sipping a cocktail*

ECQ Bar
69 Macquarie Street,
Sydney.
Tel: (02) 9256 4000
• *Relaxed, terrace-style bar
in the Quay Grand Suites,
overlooking the bustle of
Circular Quay.*

Grand Pacific Blue Room
Corner of Oxford Street
& South Dowling Street,
Paddington.
Tel: (02) 9331 7108
• *Buzzy restaurant and bar.*

The Krug Room
Level 41,
2 Chifley Square,
Sydney
Tel: (02) 9221 2500
• *Champagne and delectables
in a club atmosphere.*

Quay Bar
Customs House,
31 Alfred Street, Sydney
Tel: (02) 9251 3305
• *Elegant yet cosy bar in an
historic building on the edge of
Circular Quay.*

Sebel Townhouse
23 Elizabeth Bay Road,
Elizabeth Bay.
Tel: (02) 9358 3244
• *Bar in legendary hotel frequent-
ed by actors and musicians.*

Wine Banc
53 Martin Place,
Sydney.
Tel: (02) 9233 5399
• *A low-ceilinged cellar space
underneath Banc, the restaurant,
serving wine by the glass from
an almost endless wine list.*

• SHOPPING

Like any city, Sydney has many different shopping areas that are well worth exploring. Oxford Street, Paddington is known for its individual fashion boutiques and an increasing number of homeware stores. If it's bookshops you're after, wander over to Glebe and along Glebe Point Road and St Johns Road, and you'll find antiquarian and specialty bookstores. Queen Street, Woollahra runs off Oxford Street. Here you'll find some fashion stores (Lisa Ho and Akira amongst them), followed by antique shops that cater to every period of furnishing.

Akira Isogawa
12a Queen Street,
Woollahra.
• *Japanese designer creations
for women; intricate designs and
exquisite fabrics.*

Belinda
39 William Street,
Paddington.
• *Women's accessories in
a range of designer names.*

Collette Dinnigan
33 William Street,
Paddington.
• *Australia's own designer of drift,
ultra-feminine clothes has recently
opened a boutique in London.
Visit the place where it all started
while in Sydney.*

Dinosaur Designs
339 Oxford Street,
Paddington.
• *Small store, bursting with bright,
colourful handmade glass and
resin homeware and jewellery.*

Empire
18–20 Oxford Street
Paddington.
• *Also, check out Empire
Personal next door, which is full of
covetable things for one's person.*

Gowings
Corner of Market Street
and George Street,
319 George Street,
Darlinghurst.
• *A traditional menswear shop
stocking all the staples.*

Jinta Desert Art
154–156 Clarence Street,
Sydney,
Tel: (02) 9290 3639
• *Aboriginal art gallery.*

Orson & Blake
83–85 Queen Street,
Woollahra.
• *Downstairs is full of beautiful
furnishings and accessories for the
home; upstairs has elegant clothes
for women and men.*

Pigs in Space
3 Begg Lane,
Paddington.
• *Quirky boutique serving tea
and scones in the courtyard on
Saturdays in summer.*

The Queen Victoria Building
George Street, Sydney.
• *Top fashion names on the
ground floor, and Australian
art and gifts in the Quadrivium
gallery upstairs.*

The Strand Arcade
Between George Street
& Pitt Street Mall.
• *Three levels of fashion and
jewellery boutiques.*

Victoria Spring Designs
110 Oxford Street,
Paddington.
• *Baroque and Rococo are
two words that describe Victoria
Spring's luscious jewellery and
homewares.*

INDEX

Page numbers in *italics* refer to captions:

acknowledgments

The publishers would like to thank all those who have allowed their homes to be photographed for this book and apologise to those we were unable to include. Thanks especially go to Anna Bingemann, Thomas Hamel, Michael Love, Madeline Lester, Louise Bell, Wendy Whiteley, Nikky Twymann and The Platinum Agency.

ADDITIONAL PHOTOGRAPHS

Page 2: *One of the terraces in architect's Dale Jones Evans' inner-city apartment is devoted to an austere water feature. Black Balinese pebbles line the base, which is fed with water from a long talon-like sliver of copper pipe. A horizontal slit in the perimeter wall encourages draughts of air to be drawn in and cooled, before drifting across the living area.*

Page 4: *A converted boathouse located right on the edge of Lavender Bay commands a spectacular view encompassing Luna Park, the Sydney Harbour Bridge, and the Opera House.*

burned